Hoosier Lyrics by Eugene Field

Eugene Field was born on 2nd September 1850 in St. Louis, Missouri. His mother died when he was six and his father when he was nineteen. His academic life was not taken seriously and he preferred the life of a prankster until, in 1875, he began work as a journalist for the St. Joseph Gazette in Saint Joseph, Missouri.

In his career as a journalist he soon found a niche that suited him. His articles were light, humorous and written in a personal gossipy style that endeared him to his readership. Some were soon being syndicated to other newspapers around the States. Field soon rose to city editor of the Gazette.

Field had first published poetry in 1879, when his poem 'Christmas Treasures' appeared. This was the beginning that would eventually number over a dozen volumes. As well as verse Field published an extensive range of short stories including 'The Holy Cross' and 'Daniel and the Devil.'

In 1889 whilst the family were in London and Field himself was recovering from a bout of ill health he wrote his most famous poem; 'Lovers Lane'.

On 4th November 1895 Eugene Field Sr died in Chicago of a heart attack at the age of 45.

Index of Contents

INTRODUCTION

From whatever point of view the character of Eugene Field is seen, genius—rare and quaint presents itself in childlike simplicity. That he was a poet of keen perception, of rare discrimination, all will admit. He was a humorist as delicate and fanciful as Artemus Ward, Mark Twain, Bill Nye, James Whitcomb Riley, Opie Read, or Bret Harte in their happiest moods. Within him ran a poetic vein, capable of being worked in any direction, and from which he could, at will, extract that which his imagination saw and felt most. That he occasionally left the child-world, in which he longed to linger, to wander among the older children of men, where intuitively the hungry listener follows him into his Temple of Mirth, all should rejoice, for those who knew him not, can while away the moments imbibing the genius of his imagination in the poetry and prose here presented.

Though never possessing an intimate acquaintanceship with Field, owing largely to the disparity in our ages, still there existed a bond of friendliness that renders my good opinion of him in a measure trustworthy. Born in the same city, both students in the same college, engaged at various times in newspaper work both in St. Louis and Chicago, residents of the same ward, with many mutual friends, it is not surprising that I am able to say of him that "the world is better off that he lived, not in gold and silver or precious jewels, but in the bestowal of priceless truths, of which the possessor of this book becomes a benefactor of no mean share of his estate."

Every lover of Field, whether of the songs of childhood or the poems that lend mirth to the out-pouring of his poetic nature, will welcome this unique collection of his choicest wit and humor.

Charles Walter Brown
Chicago, January, 1905

HOOSIER LYRICS PARAPHRASED

We've come from Indiany, five hundred miles or more,
Supposin' we wuz goin' to get the nominashin, shore;
For Col. New assured us (in that noospaper o' his)
That we cud hev the airth, if we'd only tend to biz.
But here we've been a-slavin' more like bosses than like men
To diskiver that the people do not hanker arter Ben;
It is fur Jeems G. Blaine an' not for Harrison they shout—
And the gobble-uns 'el git us
Ef we
Don't
Watch

Out!

When I think of the fate that is waiting for Ben,
I pine for the peace of my childhood again;
I wish in my sorrow I could strip to the soul
And hop off once more in the old swimmin' hole!

The world is full of roses, and the roses full of dew
(Which is another word for soup) that drips for me and you.

"Little Benjy! Little Benjy!" chirps the robin in the tree;
"Little Benjy!" sighs the clover, "Little Benjy!" moans the bee;
"Little Benjy! Little Benjy!" murmurs John C. New,
A-stroking down the whiskers which the winds have whistled through.

Looks jest like his grampa, who's dead these many years—
He wears the hat his grampa wore, pulled down below his ears;
We'd like to have him four years more, but if he cannot stay—
Nothin' to say, good people; nothin' at all to say!

There, little Ben, don't cry!
They have busted your boom, I know;
And the second term
For which you squirm
Has gone where good niggers go!
But Blaine is safe, and the goose hangs high—
There, little Ben, don't cry!

Mabbe we'll git even for this unexpected shock,
When the frost is on the pumpkin and the fodder's in the shock!

Oh, the newspaper man! He works for paw;
He's the liveliest critter 'at ever you saw;
With whiskers 'at reach f'om his eyes to his throat.
He knows how to wheedle and rivet a vote;
He wunst wuz a consul 'way over the sea—
But never again a consul he'll be!
He come back f'om Lon'on one mornin' in May—
He come back for bizness, an' here he will stay—
Ain't he a awful slick newspaper man?
A newspaper, newspaper, newspaper man!

You kin talk about yer cities where the politicians meet—
You kin talk about yer cities where a decent man gits beat;
With the general run o' human kind I beg to disagree—
The little town of Tailholt is good enough f'r me!

Chicago was a pleasant town in eighteen-eighty-eight,
And I have lived in Washington long time in splendid state;
But all the present prospects are that after ninety-three
The little town o' Tailholt 'll be good enough f'r me!

"I wunst lived in Indiany," said a consul, gaunt and grim,
As most of us Blaine delegates wuz kind o' guyin' him;
"I wunst lived in Indiany, and my views wuz widely read,
Fur I run a daily paper w'ich 'Lije Halford edited;
But since I've been away f'm home, my paper (seems to me)
Ain't nearly such a inflooence ez wot it used to be;
So, havin' done with consulin', I'm goin' to make a break
Towards making of a paper like the one I used to make."

Think, if you kin, of his term mos' through,
An' that ol' man wantin' a secon' term, too;
Picture him bendin' over the form
Of his consul-gineril, stanch an' grim,
Who has stood the brunt of that jimblain storm—
An' that ol' man jest wrapt up in him!
An' the consul-gineril, with eyes all bleared
An' a haunted look in his ashen beard,
Kind o' gaspin' a feeble way—
But soothed to hear the ol' man say
In a meaning tone (as one well may
When words are handy and —'s to pay):
"Good-by, John; take care of yo'self!"

GETTIN' ON

When I wuz somewhat younger,
I wuz reckoned purty gay—
I had my fling at everything
In a rollickin', coltish way,
But times have strangely altered
Since sixty years ago—
This age of steam an' things don't seem
Like the age I used to know,
Your modern innovations
Don't suit me, I confess,
As did the ways of the good ol' days—
But I'm gettin' on, I guess.

I set on the piazza
An' hitch around with the sun—
Sometimes, mayhap, I take a nap,
Waitin' till school is done,
An' then I tell the children
The things I done in youth,
An' near as I can (as a venerable man)
I stick to the honest truth!
But the looks of them 'at listen
Seems sometimes to express

The remote idee that I'm gone—you see!
An' I am gettin' on, I guess.

I get up in the mornin',
An' nothin' else to do,
Before the rest are up and dressed
I read the papers through;
I hang 'round with the women
All day an' hear 'em talk,
An' while they sew or knit I show
The baby how to walk;
An' somehow, I feel sorry
When they put away his dress
An' cut his curls ('cause they're like a girl's)—
I'm gettin' on, I guess!

Sometimes, with twilight round me,
I see (or seem to see)
A distant shore where friends of yore
Linger and watch for me;
Sometimes I've heered 'em callin'
So tenderlike 'nd low
That it almost seemed like a dream I dreamed,
Or an echo of long ago;
An' sometimes on my forehead
There falls a soft caress,
Or the touch of a hand—you understand—
I'm gettin' on, I guess.

MINNIE LEE

Writing from an Indiana town a young woman asks: "Is the enclosed poem worth anything?"

We find that the poem is as follows:

She has left us, our own darling—
And we never more shall see
Here on earth our dearly loved one—
God has taken Minnie Lee.

Her heart was full of goodness
And her face was fair to see
And her life was full of beauty—
How we miss our Minnie Lee!

But her work on earth is over
And her spirit now is free
She has gone to live in heaven—
Shall we weep for Minnie Lee?

Would we call our angel darling
Back again across the sea?
No! but sometime up in heaven
We will meet loved Minnie Lee.

To the question as to whether this poem is worth anything we chose to answer in verse as follows:

Sweet poetess, your poetry
Is bad as bad can be,
And yet we heartily deplore
The death of Minnie Lee.

It would have pleased us better
If, in His wisdom, He
Had taken you, sweet poetess,
Instead of Minnie Lee.

Your turn will come, however,
And swift and sure 'twill be
If you continue sending
Your rhymes on Minnie Lee.

From this we hope you will gather
A dim surmise that we
Don't take much stock in poems
Concerning Minnie Lee.

LIZZIE

I wonder ef all wimmin air
Like Lizzie is when we go out
To theaters an' concerts where
Is things the papers talk about.
Do other wimmin fret and stew
Like they wuz bein' crucified—
Frettin' a show or a concert through,
With wonderin' ef the baby cried?

Now Lizzie knows that gran'ma's there
To see that everything is right,
Yet Lizzie thinks that gran'ma's care
Ain't good enuf f'r baby, quite;
Yet what am I to answer when
She kind uv fidgets at my side,
An' every now and then;
"I wonder ef the baby cried?"

Seems like she seen two little eyes

A-pinin' f'r their mother's smile—
Seems like she heern the pleadin' cries
Uv one she thinks uv all the while;
An' she's sorry that she come,
'An' though she allus tries to hide
The truth, she'd ruther stay to hum
Than wonder ef the baby cried.

Yes, wimmin folks is all alike—
By Lizzie you kin jedge the rest.
There never was a little tyke,
But that his mother loved him best,
And nex' to bein' what I be—
The husband of my gentle bride—
I'd wisht I wuz that croodlin' wee,
With Lizzie wonderin' ef I cried.

OUR LADY OF THE MINE

The Blue Horizon wuz a mine us fellers all thought well uv,
And there befell the episode I now perpose to tell uv;
'Twuz in the year of sixty-nine—somewhere along in summer—
There hove in sight one afternoon a new and curious comer;
His name wuz Silas Pettibone—an artist by perfession,
With a kit of tools and a big mustache and a pipe in his possession;
He told us, by our leave, he'd kind uv like to make some sketches
Uv the snowy peaks, 'nd the foamin' crick, 'nd the distant mountain stretches;
"You're welkim, sir," sez we, although this scenery dodge seemed to us
A waste uv time where scenery wuz already sooper-floo-us.

All through the summer Pettibone kep' busy at his sketchin'—
At daybreak, off for Eagle Pass, and home at nightfall, fetchin'
That everlastin' book uv his with spider lines all through it—
Three-Fingered Hoover used to say there warn't no meanin' to it—
"God durn a man," sez he to him, "whose shif'less hand is sot at
A-drawin' hills that's full of quartz that's pinin' to be got at!"
"Go on," sez Pettibone, "go on, if joshin' gratifies ye,
But one uv these fine times, I'll show ye sumthin' will surprise ye!"
The which remark led us to think—although he didn't say it—
That Pettibone wuz owin' us a gredge 'nd meant to pay it.

One evenin' as we sat around the restauraw de Casey,
A-singin' songs 'nd tellin' yarns the which wuz sumwhat racy,
In come that feller Pettibone 'nd sez: "With your permission
I'd like to put a picture I have made on exhibition."
He sot the picture on the bar 'nd drew aside its curtain,
Sayin': "I recken you'll allow as how that's art, f'r certain!"
And then we looked, with jaws agape, but nary word wuz spoken,

And f'r a likely spell the charm uv silence wuz unbroken—
Till presently, as in a dream, remarked Three-Fingered Hoover:
"Onless I am mistaken, this is Pettibone's shef doover!"
It wuz a face, a human face—a woman's, fair 'nd tender,
Sot gracefully upon a neck white as a swan's, and slender;
The hair wuz kind of sunny, 'nd the eyes wuz sort uv dreamy,
The mouth wuz half a-smilin', 'nd the cheeks wuz soft 'nd creamy;
It seemed like she wuz lookin' off into the west out yonder,
And seemed like, while she looked, we saw her eyes grow softer, fonder—
Like, lookin' off into the west where mountain mists wuz fallin',
She saw the face she longed to see and heerd his voice a-callin';
"Hooray!" we cried; "a woman in the camp uv Blue Horizon—
Step right up, Colonel Pettibone, 'nd nominate your pizen!"

A curious situation—one deservin' uv your pity—
No human, livin' female thing this side of Denver City!
But jest a lot uv husky men that lived on sand 'nd bitters—
Do you wonder that that woman's face consoled the lonesome critters?
And not a one but what it served in some way to remind him
Of a mother or a sister or a sweetheart left behind him—
And some looked back on happier days and saw the old-time faces
And heerd the dear familiar sounds in old familiar places—
A gracious touch of home—"Look here," sez Hoover, "ever'body
Quit thinkin' 'nd perceed at oncet to name his favorite toddy!"

It wuzn't long afore the news had spread the country over,
And miners come a-flockin' in like honey bees to clover;
It kind uv did 'em good they said, to feast their hungry eyes on
That picture uv Our Lady in the camp uv Blue Horizon.
But one mean cuss from Nigger Crick passed criticisms on 'er—
Leastwise we overheerd him call her Pettibone's madonner,
The which we did not take to be respectful to a lady—
So we hung him in a quiet spot that wuz cool 'nd dry 'nd shady;
Which same might not have been good law, but it wuz the right maneuver
To give the critics due respect for Pettibone's shef doover.

Gone is the camp—yes, years ago, the Blue Horizon busted,
And every mother's son uv us got up one day 'nd dusted,
While Pettibone perceeded east with wealth in his possession
And went to Yurrup, as I heerd, to study his perfession;
So, like as not, you'll find him now a-paintin' heads 'nd faces
At Venus, Billy Florence and the like I-talyun places—
But no such face he'll paint again as at old Blue Horizon,
For I'll allow no sweeter face no human soul sot eyes on;
And when the critics talk so grand uv Paris 'nd the loover,
I say: "Oh, but you orter seen the Pettibone shef doover!"

PENN-YAN BILL

I

In gallus old Kentucky, where the grass is very blue,
Where the liquor is the smoothest and the girls are fair and true,
Where the crop of he-gawd gentlemen is full of heart and sand,
And the stock of four-time winners is the finest in the land;
Where the democratic party in bourbon hardihood
For more than half a century unterrified has stood,
Where nod the black-eyed Susans to the prattle of the rill—
There—there befell the wooing of Penn-Yan Bill.

II

Down yonder in the cottage that is nestling in the shade
Of the walnut trees that seem to love that quiet little glade
Abides a pretty maiden of the bonny name of Sue—
As pretty as the black-eyed flow'rs and quite as modest, too;
And lovers came there by the score, of every age and kind,
But not a one (the story goes) was quite to Susie's mind.
Their sighs, their protestations, and their pleadings made her ill—
Till at once upon the scene hove Penn-Yan Bill.

III

He came from old Montana and he rode a broncho mare,
He had a rather howd'y'do and rough-and-tumble air;
His trousers were of buckskin and his coat of furry stuff—
His hat was drab of color and its brim was wide enough;
Upon each leg a stalwart boot reached just above the knee,
And in the belt about his waist his weepons carried he;
A rather strapping lover for our little Susie—still,
She was his choice and he was hers, was Penn-Yan Bill.

IV

We wonder that the ivy seeks out the oaken tree,
And twines her tendrils round him, though scarred and gnarled he be;
We wonder that a gentle girl, unused to worldly cares,
Should choose a man whose life has been a constant scrap with bears;
Ah, 'tis the nature of the vine, and of the maiden, too—
So when the bold Montana boy came from his lair to woo,
The fair Kentucky blossom felt all her heartstrings thrill
Responsive to the purring of Penn-Yan Bill.

V

He told her of his cabin in the mountains far away,

Of the catamount that howls by night, the wolf that yawps by day;
He told her of the grizzly with the automatic jaw,
He told her of the Injun who devours his victims raw;
Of the jayhawk with his tawdry crest and whiskers in his throat,
Of the great gosh-awful sarpent and the Rocky mountain goat.
A book as big as Shakespeare's or as Webster's you could fill
With the yarns that emanated from Penn-Yan Bill!

VI

Lo, as these mighty prodigies the westerner relates,
Her pretty mouth falls wide agape—her eyes get big as plates;
And when he speaks of varmints that in the Rockies grow
She shudders and she clings to him and timidly cries "Oh!"
And then says he: "Dear Susie, I'll tell you what to do—
You be my wife, and none of these 'ere things dare pester you!"
And she? She answers, clinging close and trembling yet: "I will."
And then he gives her one big kiss, does Penn-Yan Bill.

VII

Avaunt, ye poet lovers, with your wishywashy lays!
Avaunt, ye solemn pedants, with your musty, bookish ways!
Avaunt, ye smurking dandies who air your etiquette
Upon the gold your fathers worked so long and hard to get!
How empty is your nothingness beside the sturdy tales
Which mountaineers delight to tell of border hills and vales—
Of snaix that crawl, of beasts that yowl, of birds that flap and trill
In the wild egregious altitude of Penn-Yan Bill.

VIII

Why, over all these mountain peaks his honest feet have trod—
So high above the rest of us he seemed to walk with God;
He's breathed the breath of heaven, as it floated, pure and free,
From the everlasting snow-caps to the mighty western sea;
And he's heard that awful silence which thunders in the ear:
"There is a great Jehovah, and His biding place is here!"
These—these solemn voices and these the sights that thrill
In the far-away Montana of Penn-Yan Bill.

IX

Of course she had to love him, for it was her nature to;
And she'll wed him in the summer, if all we hear be true.
The blue grass will be waving in that cool Kentucky glade
Where the black-eyed Susans cluster in the pleasant walnut shade—

Where the doves make mournful music and the locust trills a song
To the brook that through the pasture scampers merrily along;
And speechless pride and rapture ineffable shall fill
The beatific bosom of Penn-Yan Bill!

ED

Ed was a man that played for keeps, 'nd when he tuk the notion,
You cudn't stop him any more'n a dam 'ud stop the ocean;
For when he tackled to a thing 'nd sot his mind plum to it,
You bet yer boots he done that thing though it broke the bank to do it!
So all us boys uz knowed him best allowed he wusn't jokin'
When on a Sunday he remarked uz how he'd gin up smokin'.
Now this remark, that Ed let fall, fell, ez I say, on Sunday—
Which is the reason we wuz shocked to see him sail in Monday
A-puffin' at a snipe that sizzled like a Chinese cracker
An' smelt fur all the world like rags instead uv like terbacker;
Recoverin' from our first surprise, us fellows fell to pokin'
A heap uv fun at "folks uz said how they had gin up smokin'."
But Ed—sez he: "I found my work cud not be done without it—
Jes' try the scheme yourself, my friends, ef any uv you doubt it!
It's hard, I know, upon one's health, but there's a certain beauty
In makin' sackerfices to the stern demand uv duty!
So, wholly in a sperrit uv denial 'nd concession
I mortify the flesh 'nd fur the sake uv my perfession!"

HOW SALTY WIN OUT

Used to think that luck wuz luck and nuthin' else but luck—
It made no diff'rence how or when or where or why it struck;
But sev'ral years ago I changt my mind and now proclaim
That luck's a kind uv science—same as any other game;
It happened out in Denver in the spring uv '80, when
Salty teched a humpback an' win out ten.

Salty wuz a printer in the good ol' Tribune days,
An', natural-like, he fell in love with the good ol' Tribune ways;
So, every Sunday evenin' he would sit into the game
Which in this crowd uv thoroughbreds I think I need not name;
An' there he'd sit until he rose, an', when he rose he wore
Invariably less wealth about his person than before.

But once there come a powerful change; one sollum Sunday night
Occurred the tidle wave what put ol' Salty out o' sight!
He win on deuce an' ace an' jack—he win on king an' queen—
Cliff Bill allowed the like uv how he win wuz never seen!

An' how he done it wuz revealed to all us fellers when
He said he teched a humpback to win out ten.

There must be somethin' in it for he never win afore,
An' when he tole the crowd about the humpback, how they swore!
For every sport allows it is a losin' game to buck
Agin the science of a man who's teched a hump f'r luck;
An' there is no denyin' luck was nowhere in it when
Salty teched a humpback an' win out ten.

I've had queer dreams an' seen queer things, an' allus tried to do
The thing that luck apparrently intended f'r me to;
Cats, funerils, cripples, beggars have I treated with regard,
An' charity subscriptions have hit me powerful hard;
But what's the use uv talkin'? I say, an' say again;
You've got to tech a humpback to win out ten!

So, though I used to think that luck wuz lucky, I'll allow
That luck, for luck, agin a hump ain't nowhere in it now!
An' though I can't explain the whys an' wherefores, I maintain
There must be somethin' in it when the tip's so straight an' plain;
For I wuz there an' seen it, an' got full with Salty when
Salty teched a humpback and win out ten!

HIS QUEEN

Our gifted and genial friend, Mr. William J. Florence, the comedian, takes to verses as naturally as a canvas-back duck takes to celery sauce. As a balladist he has few equals and no superiors, and when it comes to weaving compliments to the gentler sex he is without a peer. We find in the New York Mirror the latest verses from Mr. Florence's pen; they are entitled "Pasadene," and the first stanza flows in this wise:

I've journeyed East, I've journeyed West,
And fair Italia's fields I've seen;
But I declare
None can compare
With thee, my rose-crowned Pasadene.

Following this introduction come five stanzas heaping even more glowing compliments upon this Miss Pasadene—whoever she may be—we know her not. They are handsome compliments, beautifully phrased, yet they give us the heartache, for we know Mrs. Florence, and it grieves us to see her husband dribbling away his superb intellect in penning verses to other women. Yet we think we understand it all; these poets have a pretty way of hymning the virtues of their wives under divers aliases. So, catching the afflatus of the genial actor-poet's muse, we would answer:

Come, now, who is this Pasadene
That such a whirl of praises warrant?
And is a rose
Her only clo'es?

Oh, fie upon you, Billy Florence!

Ah, no; that's your poetic way
Of turning loose your rhythmic torrents—
This Pasadene
Is not your queen—
We know you know we know it, Florence!

So sing your songs of women folks—
We'll read without the least abhorrence,
Because we know
Through weal and woe
Your queen is Mrs. Billy Florence!

ALASKAN BALLADRY—III

(Skans in Love)

I am like the wretched seal
Wounded by a barbed device—
Helpless fellow! how I bellow,
Floundering on the jagged ice!

Sitka's beauty is the steel
That hath wrought this piteous woe:
Yet would I rather die
Than recover from the blow!

Still I'd rather live than die,
Grievous though my torment be;
Smite away, but, I pray,
Smite no victim else than me!

THE BIGGEST FISH

When, in the halcyon days of old, I was a little tyke,
I used to fish in pickerel ponds for minnows and the like;
And, oh, the bitter sadness with which my soul was fraught
When I rambled home at nightfall with the puny string I'd caught!
And, oh, the indignation and the valor I'd display
When I claimed that all the biggest fish I'd caught had got away!

Sometimes it was the rusty hooks, sometimes the fragile lines,
And many times the treacherous reeds were actually to blame.
I kept right on at losing all the monsters just the same—
I never lost a little fish—yes, I am free to say
It always was the biggest fish I caught that got away.

And so it was, when, later on, I felt ambition pass
From callow minnow joys to nobler greed for pike and bass;
I found it quite convenient, when the beauties wouldn't bite
And I returned all bootless from the watery chase at night,
To feign a cheery aspect and recount in accents gay
How the biggest fish that I had caught had somehow got away.

And, really, fish look bigger than they are before they're caught—
When the pole is bent into a bow and the slender line is taut,
When a fellow feels his heart rise up like a doughnut in his throat
And he lunges in a frenzy up and down the leaky boat!
Oh, you who've been a-fishing will indorse me when I say
That it always is the biggest fish you catch that gets away!

'Tis even so in other things—yes, in our greedy eyes
The biggest boon is some elusive, never-captured prize;
We angle for the honors and the sweets of human life—
Like fishermen we brave the seas that roll in endless strife;
And then at last, when all is done and we are spent and gray,
We own the biggest fish we've caught are those that get away.

I would not have it otherwise; 'tis better there should be
Much bigger fish than I have caught a-swimming in the sea;
For now some worthier one than I may angle for that game—
May by his arts entice, entrap, and comprehend the same;
Which, having done, perchance he'll bless the man who's proud to say
That the biggest fish he ever caught were those that got away.

BONNIE JIM CAMPBELL: A LEGISLATIVE MEMORY

Bonnie Jim Campbell rode up the glen,
But it wasn't to meet the butterine men;
It wasn't Phil Armour he wanted to see,
Nor Haines nor Crafts—though their friend was he.
Jim Campbell was guileless as man could be—
No fraud in his heart had he;
'Twas all on account of his character's sake
That he sought that distant Wisconsin lake.

Bonnie Jim Campbell came riding home,
And now he sits in the rural gloam;
A tear steals furtively down his nose
As salt as the river that yonder flows;
To the setting sun and the rising moon
He plaintively warbles the good old tune:

"Of all the drinks that ever were made—
From sherbet to circus lemonade—
Not one's so healthy and sweet, I vow,

As the rich, thick cream of the Elgin cow!
Oh, that she were here to enliven the scene,
Right merry would be our hearts, I ween;
Then, then again, Bob Wilbanks and I
Would take it by turns and milk her dry!
We would stuff her paunch with the best of hay
And milk her a hundred times a day!"

'Tis thus that Bonnie Jim Campbell sings—
A young he-angel with sprouting wings;
He sings and he prays that Fate'll allow
Him one more whack at the Elgin cow!

LYMAN, FREDERICK AND JIM

Lyman and Frederick and Jim, one day,
Set out in a great big ship—
Steamed to the ocean down to the bay
Out of a New York slip.
"Where are you going and what is your game?"
The people asked to those three.
"Darned, if we know; but all the same
Happy as larks are we;
And happier still we're going to be!"
Said Lyman
And Frederick
And Jim.

The people laughed "Aha, oho!
Oho, aha!" laughed they;
And while those three went sailing so
Some pirates steered that way.
The pirates they were laughing, too—
The prospect made them glad;
But by the time the job was through
Each of them pirates bold and bad,
Had been done out of all he had
By Lyman
And Frederick
And Jim.

Days and weeks and months they sped,
Painting that foreign clime
A beautiful, bright vermillion red—
And having a — of a time!
'Twas all so gaudy a lark, it seemed,
As if it could not be,
And some folks thought it a dream they dreamed
Of sailing that foreign sea,

But I'll identify you these three—
Lyman
And Frederick
And Jim.

Lyman and Frederick are bankers and sich
And Jim is an editor kind;
The first two named are awfully rich
And Jim ain't far behind!
So keep your eyes open and mind your tricks,
Or you are like to be
In quite as much of a Tartar fix
As the pirates that sailed the sea
And monkeyed with the pardners three,
Lyman
And Frederick
And Jim.

A WAIL

My name is Col. Johncey New,
And by a hoosier's grace
I have congenial work to do
At 12 St. Helen's place.
I was as happy as a clam
A-floating with the tide,
Till one day came a cablegram
To me from t'other side.

It was a Macedonian cry
From Benjy o'er the sea;
"Come hither, Johncey, instantly,
And whoop things up for me!"
I could not turn a callous ear
Unto that piteous cry;
I packed my grip, and for the pier
Directly started I.

Alas! things are not half so fair
As four short years ago—
The clouds are gathering everywhere
And boisterous breezes blow;
My wilted whiskers indicate
The depth of my disgrace—
Would I were back, enthroned in state,
At 12 St. Helen's place!

The saddest words, as I'll allow,
That drop from tongue or pen,

Are these sad words I utter now:
"They can't, shan't, won't have Ben!"
So, with my whiskers in my hands,
My journey I'll retrace,
To wreak revenge on foreign lands
At 12 St. Helen's place.

CLENDENIN'S LAMENT

While bridal knots are being tied
And bridal meats are being basted,
I shiver in the cold outside
And pine for joys I've never tasted.

Oh, what's a nomination worth,
When you have labored months to get it
If, all at once, with heartless mirth,
The cruel senator's upset it?

Fate weaves me such a toilsome way,
My modest wisdom may not ken it—
But, all the same, a plague I say
Upon that stingy, hostile senate!

ON THE WEDDING OF G. C

(June 2, 1886)

Oh, hand me down my spike tail coat
And reef my waistband in,
And tie this necktie round my throat
And fix my bosom pin;
I feel so weak and flustered like,
I don't know what I say—
For I am to be wedded to-day, Dan'l,
I'm to be wedded to-day!

Put double sentries at the doors
And pull the curtains down,
And tell the democratic bores
That I am out of town;
It's funny folks haint decency
Enough to stay away,
When I'm to be wedded to-day, Dan'l,
I'm to be wedded to-day!

The bride, you say, is calm and cool

In satin robes of white—
Well, I am stolid, as a rule,
But now I'm flustered quite;
Upon a surging sea of bliss
My soul is borne away,
For I'm to be wedded to-day, Dan'l,
I'm to be wedded to-day!

TO G. C.

(July 12, 1886)

They say our president has stuck
Above his good wife's door
The sign provocative of luck—
A horseshoe—nothing more.

Be hushed, O party hates, the while
That emblem lingers there,
And thou, dear fates, propitious smile
Upon the wedded pair.

I've tried the horseshoe's weird intent
And felt its potent joy—
God bless you, Mr. President,
And may it be a boy.

TO DR. F. W. R.

If I were rich enough to buy
A case of wine (though I abhor it),
I'd send a quart of extra dry
And willingly get trusted for it.
But, lackaday! You know that I'm
As poor as Job's historic turkey—
In lieu of Mumm, accept this rhyme,
An honest gift though somewhat jerky.

This is your silver wedding day—
You didn't mean to let me know it!
And yet your smiles and raiments gay
Beyond all peradventure show it!
By all you say and do it's clear
A birdling in your heart is singing,
And everywhere you go you hear
The old-time bridal bells a-ringing.

Ah, well, God grant that these dear chimes
May mind you of the sweetness only
Of those far distant, callow times
When you were Benedick and lonely—
And when an angel blessed your lot—
For angel is your helpmeet, truly—
And when, to share the joy she brought,
Came other little angels, duly.

So here's a health to you and wife—
Long may you mock the Reaper's warning,
And may the evening of your life
In rising sons renew the morning;
May happiness and peace and love
Come with each morrow to caress ye,
And when you're done with earth, above—
God bless ye, dear old friend—God bless ye!

HORACE'S ODE TO "LYDIA" ROCHE

No longer the boys,
With their music and noise,
Demand your election as mayor;
Such a milk-wagon hack
Has no place on the track
When his rival's a thoroughbred stayer.

With your coarse, shallow wit
Every rational cit
At last is completely disgusted;
The tool of the rings,
Trusts, barons, and things,
What wonder, I wonder, you're busted!

As soon as that Yerkes
Finds out you can't work his
Intrigues for the popular nickel,
With a tear to deceive you
He'll drop you and leave you
In your normal condition—a pickle.

Go, dodderer, go
Where the whisker winds blow
And spasms of penitence trouble;
Or flounder and whoop
In an ocean of soup
Where the pills of adversity bubble.

A PARAPHRASE, CIRCA 1715

Since Chloe is so monstrous fair,
With such an eye and such an air,
What wonder that the world complains
When she each am'rous suit disdains?

Close to her mother's side she clings
And mocks the death her folly brings
To gentle swains that feel the smarts
Her eyes inflict upon their hearts.

Whilst thus the years of youth go by,
Shall Colin languish, Strephon die?
Nay, cruel nymph! come, choose a mate,
And choose him ere it be too late!

A PARAPHRASE, OSTENSIBLY BY DR. I. W.

Why, Mistress Chloe, do you bother
With prattlings and with vain ado
Your worthy and industrious mother,
Eschewing them that come to woo?

Oh, that the awful truth might quicken
This stern conviction to your breast:
You are no longer now a chicken
Too young to quit the parent nest.

So put aside your froward carriage
And fix your thoughts, whilst yet there's time,
Upon the righteousness of marriage
With some such godly man as I'm.

HORACE I, 27.

In maudlin spite let Thracians fight
Above their bowls of liquor,
But such as we, when on a spree,
Should never bawl and bicker!

These angry words and clashing swords
Are quite de trop, I'm thinking;
Brace up, my boys, and hush your noise,
And drown your wrath in drinking.

Aha, 'tis fine—this mellow wine
With which our host would dope us!
Now let us hear what pretty dear
Entangles him of Opus.

I see you blush—nay, comrades, hush!
Come, friend, though they despise you,
Tell me the name of that fair dame—
Perchance I may advise you.

O wretched youth! and is it truth
You love that fickle lady?
I, doting dunce, courted her once,
And she is reckoned shady!

HEINE'S "WIDOW OR DAUGHTER"

Shall I woo the one or the other?
Both attract me—more's the pity!
Pretty is the widowed mother,
And the daughter, too, is pretty.

When I see that maiden shrinking,
By the gods, I swear I'll get 'er!
But, anon, I fall to thinking
That the mother'll suit me better!

So, like any idiot ass—
Hungry for the fragrant fodder,
Placed between two bales of grass,
Lo, I doubt, delay, and dodder!

HORACE II, 20

Maecenas, I propose to fly
To realms beyond these human portals;
No common things shall be my wings,
But such as sprout upon immortals.

Of lowly birth, once shed of earth,
Your Horace, precious (so you've told him),
Shall soar away—no tomb of clay
Nor Stygian prison house shall hold him.

Upon my skin feathers begin
To warn the songster of his fleeting;
But never mind—I leave behind

Songs all the world shall keep repeating.

Lo, Boston girls with corkscrew curls,
And husky westerns, wild and woolly,
And southern climes shall vaunt my rhymes—
And all profess to know me fully.

Methinks the west shall know me best
And therefore hold my memory dearer,
For by that lake a bard shall make
My subtle, hidden meanings clearer.

So cherished, I shall never die—
Pray, therefore, spare your dolesome praises,
Your elegies and plaintive cries,
For I shall fertilize no daisies!

HORACE'S SPRING POEM

(Odes I, 4)

The western breeze is springing up, the ships are in the bay,
And Spring has brought a happy change as Winter melts away;
No more in stall or fire the herd or plowman finds delight,
No longer with the biting frosts the open fields are white.

Our Lady of Lythera now prepares to lead the dance,
While from above the ruddy moon bestows a friendly glance;
The nymphs and comely Graces join with Venus and the choir,
And Vulcan's glowing fancy lightly turns to thoughts of fire.

Now is the time with myrtle green to crown the shining pate,
And with the early blossoms of the spring to decorate;
To sacrifice to Faunus—on whose favor we rely—
A sprightly lamb, mayhap a kid, as he may specify.

Impartially the feet of Death at huts and castles strike—
The influenza carries off the rich and poor alike;
O Sestius! though blest you are beyond the common run,
Life is too short to cherish e'en a distant hope begun.

The Shades and Pluto's mansion follow hard upon la grippe—
Once there you cannot throw at dice or taste the wine you sip,
Nor look on Lycidas, whose beauty you commend,
To whom the girls will presently their courtesies extend.

HORACE TO LIGURINE

(Odes IV, 10)

O cruel fair,
Whose flowing hair
The envy and the pride of all is,
As onward roll
The years, that poll
Will get as bald as a billiard ball is;
Then shall your skin, now pink and dimply,
Be tanned to parchment, sear and pimply!

When you behold
Yourself grown old
These words shall speak your spirits moody:
"Unhappy one!
What heaps of fun
I've missed by being goody-goody!
Oh! that I might have felt the hunger
Of loveless age when I was younger!"

HORACE ON HIS MUSCLE

(Epode VI)

You (blatant coward that you are!)
Upon the helpless vent your spite;
Suppose you ply your trade on me—
Come, monkey with this bard and see
How I'll repay your bark with bite!

Ay, snarl just once at me, you brute!
And I shall hound you far and wide,
As fiercely as through drifted snow
The shepherd dog pursues what foe
Skulks on the Spartan mountain side!

The chip is on my shoulder, see?
But touch it and I'll raise your fur;
I'm full of business; so beware,
For, though I'm loaded up for bear,
I'm quite as likely to kill a cur!

HORACE TO MAECENAS

(Odes III, 29)

Dear noble friend! a virgin cask
Of wine solicits attention—
And roses fair, to deck your hair,
And things too numerous to mention,
So tear yourself awhile away
From urban turmoil, pride and splendor
And deign to share what humble fare
And sumptuous fellowship I tender;
The sweet content retirement brings
Smoothes out the ruffled front of kings.

The evil planets have combined
To make the weather hot and hotter—
By parboiled streams the shepherd dreams
Vainly of ice-cream soda-water;
And meanwhile you, defying heat,
With patriotic ardor ponder
On what old Rome essays at home
And what her heathen do out yonder.
Maecenas, no such vain alarm
Disturbs the quiet of this farm!

God in his providence observes
The goal beyond this vale of sorrow,
And smiles at men in pity when
They seek to penetrate the morrow.
With faith that all is for the best,
Let's bear what burdens are presented,
That we shall say, let come what may,
"We die, as we have lived, contented!
Ours is to-day; God's is the rest—
He doth ordain who knoweth best!"

Dame Fortune plays me many a prank—
When she is kind, oh! how I go it!
But if, again, she's harsh, why, then
I am a very proper poet!
When favoring gales bring in my ships,
I hie to Rome and live in clover—
Elsewise, I steer my skiff out here,
And anchor till the storm blows over.
Compulsory virtue is the charm
Of life upon the Sabine farm!

HORACE IN LOVE AGAIN

(Epode XI)

Dear Pettius, once I reeled off rhyme

Satiric, sad and tender,
But now my quill
Has lost its skill
And I am dying in my prime
Through love of female gender!
Nay, do not laugh
Nor deign to chaff
Your friend with taunts of Lyde
And other dames
Who've been my flames—
This time it's bona-fide!

I maunder sadly to and fro—
I who was once so jolly!
My old time chums
Gyrate their thumbs
And taunt me, as I sighing go,
With what they term my folly.
I told you once,
Lake a garrulous dunce,
Of my all consuming passion,
And I rolled my eyes
In tragedy wise
And raved in lovesick fashion.

And when I'd aired my woes profound
You volunteered this warning:
"Horace, go light
On the bowl to-night—
Ten hours of sleep will bring you round
All right to-morrow morning!"
Now ten hours sleep
May do a heap
For callow hearts a-patter,
But I tell you, sir,
This affair du coeur
Of mine is a serious matter!

"GOOD-BY—GOD BLESS YOU!"

I like the Anglo-Saxon speech
With its direct revealings—
It takes a hold and seems to reach
Way down into your feelings;
That some folk deem it rude, I know,
And therefore they abuse it;
But I have never found it so—
Before all else I choose it.
I don't object that men should air

The Gallic they have paid for—
With "au revoir," "adieu, ma chere"—
For that's what French was made for—
But when a crony takes your hand
At parting to address you,
He drops all foreign lingo and
He says: "Good-by—God bless you!"

This seems to me a sacred phrase
With reverence impassioned—
A thing come down from righteous days,
Quaintly but nobly fashioned;
It well becomes an honest face—
A voice that's round and cheerful;
It stays the sturdy in his place
And soothes the weak and fearful.
Into the porches of the ears
It steals with subtle unction
And in your heart of hearts appears
To work its gracious function;
And all day long with pleasing song
It lingers to caress you—
I'm sure no human heart goes wrong
That's told "Good-by—God bless you!"

I love the words—perhaps because,
When I was leaving mother,
Standing at last in solemn pause
We looked at one another,
And—I saw in mother's eyes
The love she could not tell me—
A love eternal as the skies,
Whatever fate befell me;
She put her arms about my neck
And soothed the pain of leaving,
And, though her heart was like to break,
She spoke no word of grieving;
She let no tear bedim her eye,
For fear that might distress me,
But, kissing me, she said good-by
And asked her God to bless me.

HORACE

(Epode XIV)

You ask me, friend,
Why I don't send
The long since due-and-paid-for numbers—

Why, songless, I
As drunken lie
Abandoned to Lethæan slumbers.

Long time ago
(As well you know)
I started in upon that carmen;
My work was vain—
But why complain?
When gods forbid, how helpless are men!

Some ages back,
The sage Anack
Courted a frisky Samian body,
Singing her praise
In metered phrase
As flowing as his bowls of toddy.

'Till I was hoarse
Might I discourse
Upon the cruelties of Venus—
'Twere waste of time
As well of rhyme,
For you've been there yourself, Maecenas!

Perfect your bliss,
If some fair miss
Love you yourself and not your minæ;
I, fortune's sport,
All vainly court
The beauteous, polyandrous Phryne!

HORACE I, 23

Chloe, you shun me like a hind
That, seeking vainly for her mother,
Hears danger in each breath of wind
And wildly darts this way and t'other.

Whether the breezes sway the wood
Or lizards scuttle through the brambles,
She starts, and off, as though pursued,
The foolish, frightened creature scrambles.

But, Chloe, you're no infant thing
That should esteem a man an ogre—
Let go your mother's apron-string
And pin your faith upon a toga!

A PARAPHRASE

How happens it, my cruel miss,
You're always giving me the mitten?
You seem to have forgotten this:
That you no longer are a kitten!

A woman that has reached the years
Of that which people call discretion
Should put aside all childish fears
And see in courtship no transgression.

A mother's solace may be sweet,
But Hymen's tenderness is sweeter,
And though all virile love be meet,
You'll find the poet's love is metre.

A PARAPHRASE BY CHAUCER

Syn that you, Chloe, to your moder sticken,
Maketh all ye yonge bacheloures full sicken;
Like as a lyttel deere you been y-hiding
Whenas come lovers with theyre pityse chiding,
Sothly it ben faire to give up your moder
For to beare swete company with some oder;
Your moder ben well enow so farre shee goeth,
But that ben not farre enow, God knoweth;
Wherefore it ben sayed that foolysh ladyes
That marrye not shall leade an aype in Hayde;
But all that do with gode men wed full quicklye
When that they be on dead go to ye seints full sickerly.

HORACE I, 5

What perfumed, posie-dizened sirrah,
With smiles for diet,
Clasps you, O fair but faithless Pyrrha,
On the quiet?
For whom do you bind up your tresses,
As spun-gold yellow—
Meshes that go with your caresses,
To snare a fellow?

How will he rail at fate capricious,
And curse you duly;

Yet now he deems your wiles delicious—
You perfect truly!
Pyrrha, your love's a treacherous ocean—
He'll soon fall in there!
Then shall I gloat on his commotion,
For I have been there!

HORACE I, 20

Than you, O valued friend of mine!
A better patron non est—
Come, quaff my home-made Sabine wine—
You'll find it poor but honest.

I put it up that famous day
You patronized the ballet
And the public cheered you such a way
As shook your native valley.

Cæcuban and the Calean brand
May elsewhere claim attention,
But I have none of these on hand—
For reasons I'll not mention.

ENVOY

So come! though favors I bestow
Can not be called extensive,
Who better than my friend should know
That they're, at least, expensive!

HORACE II, 7

Pompey, what fortune gives you back
To the friends and the gods who love you—
Once more you stand in your native land,
With your native sky above you!
Ah, side by side, in years agone,
We've faced tempestuous weather,
And often quaffed
The genial draft
From an amphora together!

When honor at Phillippi fell
A pray to brutal passion,
I regret to say that my feet ran away

In swift Iambic fashion;
You were no poet-soldier born,
You staid, nor did you wince then—
Mercury came
To my help, which same
Has frequently saved me since then.

But now you're back, let's celebrate
In the good old way and classic—
Come, let us lard our skins with nard
And bedew our souls with Massic!
With fillets of green parsley leaves
Our foreheads shall be done up,
And with song shall we
Protract our spree
Until the morrow's sun-up.

HORACE I, 11

Seek not, Lucome, to know how long you're going to live yet—
What boons the gods will yet withhold, or what they're going to give yet;
For Jupiter will have his way, despite how much we worry—
Some will hang on for many a day and some die in a hurry,
The wisest thing for you to do is to embark this diem
Upon a merry escapade with some such bard as I am;
And while we sport, I'll reel you off such odes as shall surprise ye—
To-morrow, when the headache comes—well, then I'll satirize ye!

HORACE I, 13

When, Lydia, you (once fond and true,
But now grown cold and supercilious)
Praise Telly's charms of neck and arms—
Well, by the dog! it makes me bilious!

Then, with despite, my cheeks wax white,
My doddering brain gets weak and giddy,
My eyes o'erflow with tears which show
That passion melts my vitals, Liddy!

Deny, false jade, your escapade,
And, lo! your wounded shoulders show it!
No manly spark left such a mark—
(Leastwise he surely was no poet!)

With savage buss did Telephus
Abraid your lips, so plump and mellow—

As you would save what Venus gave,
I charge you shun that awkward fellow!

And now I say thrice happy they
That call on Hymen to requite 'em;
For, though love cools, the wedded fools
Must cleave 'till death doth disunite 'em!

HORACE IV, 1

O Mother Venus, quit, I pray,
Your violent assailing;
The arts, forsooth, that fired my youth
At last are unavailing—
My blood runs cold—I'm getting old
And all my powers are failing!

Speed thou upon thy white swan's wings
And elsewhere deign to mellow
With my soft arts the anguished hearts
Of swain that writhe and bellow;
And right away, seek out, I pray,
Young Paullus—he's your fellow.

You'll find young Paullus passing fate,
Modest, refined, and toney—
Go, now, incite the favored wight!
With Venus for a crony.
He'll outshine all at feast and ball
And conversazione!

Then shall that godlike nose of thine
With perfumes be requited,
And then shall prance in Salian dance
The girls and boys delighted,
And, while the lute blends with the flute,
Shall tender loves be blighted.

But as for me—as you can see—
I'm getting old and spiteful;
I have no mind to female kind
That once I deemed delightful—
No more brim up the festive cup
That sent me home at night full.

Why do I falter in my speech,
O cruel Ligurine?
Why do I chase from place to place
In weather wet and shiny?

Why down my nose forever flows
The tear that's cold and briny?

HORACE TO HIS PATRON

Mæcenas, you're of noble line—
(Of which the proof convincing
Is that you buy me all my wine
Without so much as wincing.)

To different men of different minds
Come different kinds of pleasure;
There's Marshall Field—what joy he finds
In shears and cloth-yard measure!

With joy Prof. Swing is filled
While preaching godly sermons;
With bliss is Hobart Taylor thrilled
When he is leading germans.

While Uncle Joe Medill prefers
To run a daily paper,
To Walter Gresham it occurs
That law's the proper caper.

With comedy a winning card,
How blithe is Richard Hooley;
Per contra, making soap and lard,
Rejoices Fairbank duly.

While Armour in the sugar ham
His summum bonum reaches,
MacVeagh's as happy as a clam
In canning pears and peaches.

Let Farwell glory in the fray
Which party hate increases—
His son-in-law delights to play
Gavottes and such like pieces.

So each betakes him to his task—
So each his hobby nurses—
While I—well, all the boon I ask
Is leave to write my verses.

Give, give that precious boon to me
And I shall envy no man;
If not the noblest I shall be
At least the happiest Roman!

THE "ARS POETICA" OF HORACE—XVIII

(Lines 323-333)

The Greeks had genius—'twas a gift
The Muse vouchsafed in glorious measure;
The boon of Fame they made their aim
And prized above all worldly treasure.

But we—how do we train our youth?
Not in the arts that are immortal,
But in the greed for gains that speed
From him who stands at Death's dark portal.

Ah, when this slavish love of gold
Once binds the soul in greasy fetters,
How prostrate lies—how droops and dies
The great, the noble cause of letters!

HORACE I, 34

I have not worshiped God, my King—
Folly has led my heart astray;
Backward I turn my course to learn
The wisdom of a wiser way.

How marvelous is God, the King!
How do His lightnings cleave the sky—
His thundering car spreads fear afar,
And even hell is quaked thereby!

Omnipotent is God, our King!
There is no thought He hath not read,
And many a crown His hand plucks down
To place it on a worthier head!

HORACE I, 33

Not to lament that rival flame
Wherewith the heartless Glycera scorns you,
Nor waste your time in maudlin rhyme,
How many a modern instance warns you.

Fair-browed Lycoris pines away

Because her Cyrus loves another;
The ruthless churl informs the girl
He loves her only as a brother.

For he, in turn, courts Pholoe—
A maid unscotched of love's fierce virus—
Why, goats will mate with wolves they hate
Ere Pholoe will mate with Cyrus!

Ah, weak and hapless human hearts—
By cruel Mother Venus fated
To spend this life in hopeless strife,
Because incongruously mated!

Such torture, Albius, is my lot;
For, though a better mistress wooed me,
My Myrtale has captured me
And with her cruelties subdued me!

THE "ARS POETICA" OF HORACE—I

(Lines 1-23)

Should painters attach to a fair human head
The thick, turgid neck of a stallion,
Or depict a spruce lass with the tail of a bass—
I am sure you would guy the rapscallion!

Believe me, dear Pisos, that such a freak
Is the crude and preposterous poem
Which merely abounds in a torrent of sounds
With no depth of reason below 'em.

'Tis all very well to give license to art—
The wisdom of license defend I;
But the line should be drawn at the fripperish sprawn
Of a mere cacoethes scribendi.

It is too much the fashion to strain at effects—
Yes, that's what's the matter with Hannah!
Our popular taste by the tyros debased
Paints each barnyard a grove of Diana!

Should a patron require you to paint a marine,
Would you work in some trees with their barks on?
When his strict orders are for a Japanese jar,
Would you give him a pitcher like Clarkson?

Now this is my moral: Compose what you may,

And fame will be ever far distant,
Unless you combine with a simple design
A treatment in toto consistent.

THE GREAT JOURNALIST IN SPAIN

Good Editor Dana—God bless him, we say!
Will soon be afloat on the main,
Will be steaming away
Through the mist and the spray
To the sensuous climate of Spain.

Strange sights shall he see in that beautiful land
Which is famed for its soap and Moor,
For, as we understand,
The scenery is grand,
Though the system of railway is poor.

For moonlight of silver and sunlight of gold
Glint the orchards of lemons and mangoes,
And the ladies, we're told,
Are a joy to behold
As they twine in their lissome fandangoes.

What though our friend Dana shall twang a guitar
And murmur a passionate strain—
Oh, fairer by far
Than these ravishments are
The castles abounding in Spain!

These castles are built as the builder may list—
They are sometimes of marble or stone,
But they mostly consist
Of east wind and mist
With an ivy of froth overgrown.

A beautiful castle our Dana shall raise
On a futile foundation of hope,
And its glories shall blaze
In the somnolent haze
Of the mythical lake del y Soap.

The fragrance of sunflowers shall swoon on the air,
And the visions of dreamland obtain,
And the song of "World's Fair"
Shall be heard everywhere
Through that beautiful castle in Spain.

REID, THE CANDIDATE

I saw a brave compositor
Go hustling o'er the mead,
Who bore a banner with these words:
"Hurrah for Whitelaw Reid!"

"Where go you, brother slug," I asked,
"With such unusual speed?"
He quoth: "I go to dump my vote
For gallant Whitelaw Reid!"

"But what has Whitelaw done," I asked,
"That now he should succeed?"
Said he: "The stanchest, truest friend
We have is Whitelaw Reid!

"There are no terms we can suggest
That he will not concede;
He is converted to our faith,
Is gallant Whitelaw Reid!

"The union it must be preserved—
That is this convert's creed,
And that is why we're whooping up
The cause of Whitelaw Reid!"

"If what you say of him be sooth,
You have a friend indeed,
So go on your winding way," quoth I,
"And whoop for Whitelaw Reid!"

So on unto the polls I saw
That printer straight proceed
While other printers swarmed in swarms
To vote for Whitelaw Reid.

A VALENTINE

Four little sisters standing in a row—
Which of them I love best I really do not know.
Sometimes it is the sister dressed out so fine in blue,
And sometimes she who flaunts the beauteous robe of emerald hue;
Sometimes for her who wears the brown my tender heart has bled,
And then again I am consumed of love for her in red.
So now I think I'll send this valentine unto the four—
I love them all so very much—how could a man do more?

KISSING-TIME

'Tis when the lark goes soaring,
And the bee is at the bud,
When lightly dancing zephyrs
Sing over field and flood;
When all sweet things in Nature
Seem joyfully a-chime—
'Tis then I wake my darling,
For it is kissing-time!

Go, pretty lark, a-soaring,
And suck your sweets, O bee;
Sing, O ye winds of summer,
Your songs to mine and me.
For with your song and rapture
Cometh the moment when
It is half-past kissing-time
And time to kiss again!

So—so the days go fleeting
Like golden fancies free,
And every day that cometh
Is full of sweets for me;
And sweetest are those moments
My darling comes to climb
Into my lap to mind me
That it is kissing-time.

Sometimes, may be, he wanders
A heedless, aimless way—
Sometimes, may be, he loiters
In pretty, prattling play;
But presently bethinks him
And hastens to me then,
For it's half-past kissing time
And time to kiss again!

THE FIFTH OF JULY

The sun climbs up, but still the tyrant Sleep
Holds fast our baby boy in his embrace;
The slumb'rer sighs, anon athwart his face
Faint, half-suggested frowns like shadows creep,
One little hand lies listless on his breast,
One little thumb sticks up with mute appeal,
While motley burns and powder marks reveal

The fruits of boyhood's patriotic zest.

Our baby's faithful poodle crouches near—
He, too, is weary of the din and play
That come with glorious Independence Day,
But which, thank God! come only once a year!
And Fido, too, has suffered in this cause,
Which once a year right noisily obtains,
For Fido's tail—or what thereof remains—
Is not so fair a sight as once it was.

PICNIC-TIME

It's June agin, an' in my soul I feel the fillin' joy
That's sure to come this time o' year to every little boy;
For, every June, the Sunday schools at picnics may be seen,
Where "fields beyont the swellin' floods stand dressed in livin' green."
Where little girls are skeered to death with spiders, bugs an' ants,
An' little boys get grass-stains on their go-to-meetin' pants.
It's June agin, an' with it all what happiness is mine—
There's goin' to be a picnic an' I'm goin' to jine!

One year I jined the Baptists, an' goodness! how it rained!
(But grampa says that that's the way "Baptizo" is explained.)
And once I jined the 'piscopils an' had a heap o' fun—
But the boss of all the picnics was the Presbyterium!
They had so many puddin's, sallids, sandwidges an' pies,
That a feller wisht his stummick was as hungry as his eyes!
Oh, yes, the eatin' Presbyteriums give yer is so fine
That when they have a picnic, you bet I'm goin' to jine!

But at this time the Methodists have special claims on me,
For they're goin' to give a picnic on the 21st, D. V.;
Why should a liberal Universalist like me object
To share the joys of fellowship with every friendly sect?
However het'rodox their articles of faith elsewise may be,
Their doctrine of fried chick'n is a savin' grace to me!
So on the 21st of June, the weather bein' fine,
They're goin' to give a picnic, and I'm goin' to jine!

THE ROMANCE OF A WATCH

One day his father said to John:
"Come here and see what I hev bought—
A Waterbury watch, my son—
It is the boon you long hev sought!"

The boy could scarcely believe his eyes—
The watch was shiny, smooth an' slick—
He snatched the nickel-plated prize
An' wound away to hear it tick.

He wound an' wound, an' wound an' wound,
An' kept a windin' fit to kill—
The weeks an' months an' years rolled round,
But John he kep' a windin', still!

As autumns came an' winters went
An' summers follered arter spring,
John didn't mind—he was intent
On windin' up that darned ol' thing.

He got to be a poor ol' man—
He's bald an' deaf an' blind an' lame,
But, like he did when he began,
He keeps on windin', jest the same!

OUR BABY

'Tis very strange, but quite as true,
That when our Baby smiles
Our club gets walloped black and blue
In all the latest styles;
But when our Baby's hopping mad
It's quite the other way—
Chicago beats the Yankees bad
When Baby doesn't play.

When baby stands upon his base,
Just after having kicked,
Upon his Scandinavian face
Appears the legend, "Licked";
But when he orders out a sub,
We well may hip-hooray—
Chicago has the winning club
When Baby doesn't play.

But, if our Baby's getting old,
And stiff, and cross, and vain,
And if his days are nearly told,
Oh, let us not complain.
Let's rather think of what he was
And how he's made it pay
To hire the kids that win because
Our Baby doesn't play.

THE COLOR THAT SUITS ME BEST

Any color—so long as it's red—
Is the color that suits me best,
Though I will allow there is much to be said
For yellow and green and the rest;
But the feeble tints, which some affect
In the things they make or buy,
Have never (I say it with all respect)
Appealed to my critical eye.

There's that in red that warmeth the blood
And quickeneth a man within,
And bringeth to speedy and perfect bud
The germs of original sin;
So, though I am properly born and bred,
I'll own, with a certain zest,
That any color—so long as it's red—
Is the color that suits me best!

For where is a color that can be compared
With the blush of a buxom lass—
Or where such warmth as of the hair
Of the genuine white horse class?
And, lo, reflected in this cup
Of cherry Bordeaux I see
What inspiration girdeth me up—
Yes, red is the color for me!

Through acres and acres of art I've strayed
In Italy, Germany, France;
On many a picture a master has made
I've squandered a passing glance;
Marines I hate, madonnas and
Those Dutch freaks I detest!
But the peerless daubs of my native land—
They're red, and I like them best!

'Tis little I care how folks deride—
I'm backed by the west, at least,
And we are free to say that we can't abide
The tastes that obtain down east;
And we are mighty proud to have it said
That here in the critical west,
Most any color—so long as it's red—
Is the color that suits us best!

HOW TO "FILL"

It is understood that our esteemed Col. Franc B. Wilkie is going to formulate a reply to Mrs. Ella Wheeler Wilcox's latest poem, which begins as follows:

"I hold it as a changeless law
From which no soul can sway or swerve,
We have that in us which will draw
Whate'er we need or most deserve."

We fancy the genial colonel will start off with some such quatrain as this:

"I fain would have your recipe,
If you'll but give the snap away;
Now when four clubs are dealt to me,
How may I draw another, pray?"

POLITICS IN 1888

The Cleveland Leader must be getting ready for the campaign of 1888. We find upon its editorial page quite a pretentious poem, entitled "Alpha and Omega," and here is a sample stanza:

"Whose name will stand for coming time
As hypocrites in prose and rhyme,
And be despised in every clime?
The Mugwumps."

Well, may be so, but may we be permitted to add a stanza which seems to us to be very pertinent just now?

And who next year, we'd like to know,
Will feed the Cleveland Leader crow,
Just as they did three years ago?
The Mugwumps.

THE BASEBALL SCORE

A boy came racing down the street
In a most tumultuous way,
And he hollered at all he chanced to meet:
"Hooray, hooray, hooray!"
His eyes and his breath were hot with joy
And his cheeks were all aflame—
'Twas a rare event with the little boy
When the champions won a game!

"Twenty to 6" and "10 to 2"

Were rather dismal scores,
And they wreathed in a somewhat somber hue
These classic western shores;
We shuddered and winced at the cruel sport
And our heads were bowed in shame
'Till Somewhere sent us the glad report
That the champions won the game!

Our Baby says it'll be all right
For the champions by and by,
And the twin emotions of Hope and Fright
Gleam in his cod fish eye;
And Spalding says (in his modest way)
That we'll get there all the same;
So let us holler, "Hooray, hooray,"
When the champions win the game.

CHICAGO NEWSPAPER LIFE

It pleases us to observe that the shocking habit of hurling opprobrious epithets at each other has been abandoned by the venerable editor of the Journal and the venerable editor of the Tribune. At this moment we are reminded of the inspired lines of the eminent but now, alas! Neglected Watts:

"Birds in their nests agree,
And 'tis a shocking sight
When folks, who should harmonious be,
Fall out and chide and fight.

"The tones of Andy and of Joe
Should join in friendly games—
Not be debased to vice so low
As that of calling names.

"Bad names and naughty names require
To be chastized at school,
But he's in danger of hell-fire
Who talks of 'crank' and 'fool.'

"Oh 'tis a dreadful thing to see
The old folks smite and jaw,
But pleasant it is to agree
On the election law.

"Let Joe and Andy leave their wrongs
For sinners to contest;
So shall they some time swell the songs
Of Israel's ransomed blest."

THE MIGHTY WEST

Oh, where abides the fond kazoo,
The barrel-organ fair,
And where is heard the tra-la-loo
Of fish horns on the air?
And where are found the fife and drum
Discoursed with goodliest zest?
And where do fiddles liveliest hum?
The west—the mighty west!

Sonatas, fugues, and all o' that
Are rightly judged effete,
While largos written in B-flat
Are clearly out of date;
Some like the cold pianny-forty,
But whistling suits us best—
And op'ry, if it isn't naughty,
Will not catch on out west.

From skinning hogs or canning beef
Or diving into stocks,
Could we expect to find relief
In Haydns or in Bachs?
Ah, no; from pork and wheat and lard
We turn aside with zest
To sing some opus of some bard
Whose home is in the west.

So get ye gone, ye weakling crew!
Your tunes are stale and flat,
And cannot hold a candle to
The works of Silas Pratt!
His opuses are in demand
And are the final test
By which all others fall or stand
In this the mighty west!

APRIL

Now April with sweet showers of freshening rain
Has roused last summer's vigorous breath once more;
'Tis in the air, the house, the street, the lane—
Puffs through the walls and oozes through the floor.

The rau-cous-throated frog ayont the sty
Sends forth, as erst, his amerous vermal croak,
Each hungry mooly casts her swivel eye

For pots and pails in which her nose to poke.

With gurgling glee the gutter gushes by,
Fraught all with filth, unknown and nameless dirt—
A dead green goose, an o'er-ripe rat I spy;
Head of a cat, tail of a flannel shirt.

The querulous cry of every gabbling goose
From thousand-scented mudholes echoes o'er;
The dogs and yawling cats have gotten loose
And mock the hideous howls of hell once more.

By yon scrub oak, where roots the sallow sow,
In where John Murphy's wife outpours her slop;
Right there you'll find there's almost stench now
To cause the world its nostrils to estop.

And yonder dauntless goat that bank adown,
That wreathes his old fantastic horns so high,
Gnaws sadly on the bustle of Miss Brown,
Which she discarded in the months gone by.

So in Goose Island cometh April round;
Full eagerly we watch the month's approach—
The season of sweet sight and pleasant sound,
The season of the bedbug and the roach.

REPORT OF THE BASEBALL GAME

It was a very pleasant game,
And there was naught of grumbling
Until the baleful tidings came
That Williamson was "fumbling."
Then all at once a hideous gloom
Fell o'er all manly features,
And Clayton's cozy, quiet room
Was full of frantic creatures.

"Click, click," the tiny ticker went,
The tape began to rattle,
And pallid, eager faces bent
To read the news from battle;
Down, down, ten million feet or more,
Chicago's hope went tumbling,
When came the word that Burns and Gore
And Pfeffer, too, were "fumbling."

No diagram was needed then
To point the Browns to glory—

The simple fact that these four men
Were "fumbling" told the story.
There is not a club in all the land—
No odds how weak or humble—
That beats us when our short-stop and
Our second baseman "fumble."

There was some talk of hippodrome
'Mid frequent calls for liquor,
Then each Chicago man went home
Much wiser, poorer, sicker;
And many a giant intellect
Seemed slowly, surely crumbling
Beneath the dolorous effect
Of that St. Louis "fumbling."

Ah, well, the struggle's but just begun,
So what is the use of fretting
If by a little harmless fun
Our boys can bull the betting?
When comes the tug of war there'll be
No accidental stumbling,
And then, you bet your boots, you'll see
No mention made of "fumbling."

THE ROSE

Since the days of old Adam the welkin has rung
With the praises of sweet scented posies,
And poets in rapturous phrases have sung
The paramount beauties of roses.

Wheresoever she bides, whether nestling in lanes
Or gracing the proud urban bowers,
The red, royal rose her distinction maintains
As the one regnant queen among flowers.

How joyous are we of the west when we find
That Fate, with her gifts ever chary,
Has decreed that the Rose, who is queen of her kind
Shall bloom on our wild western prairie.

Let us laugh at the east as an impotent thing
With envy and jealously crazy,
While grateful Chicago is happy to sing
In the praise of the rose—she's a daisy.

KANSAS CITY VS. DETROIT

A rooster flapped his wings and crowed
A merrysome cockadoodledoo,
As out of the west a cowboy rode
To the land where the peach and the clapboard grew,
Humming a gentle tralalaloo.

"O insect with the gilded wing,"
The cowboy cried, "Pray tell me true
Why do you crane your neck and sing
That wearisome cockadoodledoo?
Would you like to learn the tralalaloo?"

Now the rooster squawked an impudent word
Whereat the angered cowboy threw
His lariat at the haughty bird
And choked him until his gills were blue
And his eyes hung out an inch or two.

"Now hear me sing," the cowboy cried;
"It ain't no cockadoodledoo—
It's a song we sing on the prairies wide—
The simple song of tralalaloo,
Which is cowboy slang for 12 to 2."

ME AND BILKAMMLE

I will, if you choose,
Impart you some news
That will greatly astound you, I know;
You would never suspect
My ambition was wreck'd
'Till you heard my confession of woe.
'Tis not that my boom
Has ascended the flume—
In other words, gone up the spout—
I could smile a sweet smile
This tempestuous while,
But me and Bilkammle are out!

Being timid and shrinkin',
He did all the thinkin',
When I did the talkin' worth mention;
'Twas my constant ambition
To soar to position
So I gave it exclusive attention;
And supposin' that he
Would of course be for me,

I rambled and prattled about
'Till I found to my horror,
Vexation, and sorror,
That me and Bilkammle were out.

As I tore my red hair
In a fit of despair
I heard my Achates complain
That the gent with the coffer
Had nothing to offer
In the way of relieving his pain!

If there's mortal to blame
For this villainous game
Which has snuffed a great man beyond doubt.
It's that treacherous mammal
Entitled Bilkammle—
Which accounts for us two bein' out!

TO THE DETROIT BASEBALL CLUB

You've scooped the vealy city crowd
Of glory and of purse—
Why shouldn't Pegasus be proud
To trot you out in a verse?
Chicago hoped to wallop you
By a tremendous score,
But bit off more than it could chew,
As witness: "5 to 4."

Well done, you 'Ganders! here's a hand
To every one of you;
These record-breakers of the land
Now break themselves in two.
Well get their pennant—it shall float
Upon our distant shore,
So let each patriotic throat
Hurrah for "5 to 4."

A BALLAD OF ANCIENT OATHS

Ther ben a knyght, Sir Hoten hight,
That on a time did swere
In mighty store othes mickle sore,
Whiche grieved his wiffe to here.

Soth, whenne she scoft, his wiffe did oft

Swere as a lady may;
"I'faith," "I'sooth," or "lawk" in truth
Ben alle that wiffe wold say.

Soe whenne her good man waxed him wood
She mervailed much to here
The hejeous sound of othes full round
The which her lord did swere.

"Now, pray thee, speke and tell me eke
What thing hath vexed thee soe?"
The wiffe she cried; but he replied
By swereing moe and moe.

Her sweren zounds which be Gog's wounds,
By bricht Marie and Gis,
By sweit Sanct Ann and holie Tan
And by Bryde's bell, ywis.

By holie grails, by 'slids and 'snails,
By old Sanct Dunstan bauld,
The virgin faire that him did beare,
By him that Judas sauld;

By Arthure's sword, by Paynim horde,
By holie modyr's teir,
By Cokis breath, by Zooks and 's death,
And by Sanct Swithen deir;

By divells alle, both greate and smalle,
And in hell there be,
By bread and salt, and by Gog's malt,
And by the blody tree;

By Him that worn the crown of thorn
And by the sun and mone,
By deir Sanct Blanc and Sanct Fillane,
And three kings of Cologne;

By the gude Lord and His sweit word,
By him that herryit hell,
By blessed Jude, by holie rude,
And eke be Gad himsell!

He sweren soe (and mickle moe)
It made man's flesch to creepen,
The air ben blue with his ado
And sore his wiffe ben wepen.

Giff you wold know why sweren soe
The goodman high Sir Hoten,

He ben full wroth, because, in soth,
He leesed his coler boten.

AN OLD SONG REVISED

John Hamilton, my Jo John,
When first we were acquaint
You were as lavish as could be
With your vermillion paint;
But now the head that once was red
Seems veiled in sable woe,
And clouds of gloom obscure your boom,
John Hamilton, my Jo.

Oh, was it Campbell's hatchet wrought
The ruin we deplore?
Or was it Abnor Taylor's thirst
For your abundant gore?
Or was it Hank's ambitious pranks
That laid our idol low?
Come, let us know how came you so,
John Hamilton, my Joe!

We pine to know the awful truth.
So, pray, be pleased to tell
The story—full of tragic fire—
How one great statesman fell;
How dives' hand stalked in the land
And dealt a crushing blow
At one proud name—which you're the same,
John Hamilton, my Jo!

THE GRATEFUL PATIENT

The doctor leaned tenderly over the bed
And looked at the patient 's complexion,
And felt of the pulse and the feverish head,
Then stood for a time in reflection.
"A strange complication!
My recommendation
Is morphia by hypodermic injection."

The patient looked up with a leer in his eye
And winked in the doctor's direction—
"Well, Doc," he remarked, "since you say I must die,
I'm grateful to you for protection—
I'm now in position

To ask the commission
T' excuse me from serving as judge of election."

THE BEGINNING AND THE END

Death
In my breath,
Cried I then:
"Men
Burn and blight!
Nourish crime!
Scale the height!
Climb, men, climb!
Climb and fight!
Win by might!
Wrong or right!
Blood!"

Well
In a cell
Here I am—
D—n!
From my flight
So sublime
I alight
Ere my time,
And in fright
Here I grope
Through the night
Without hope.
What a plight!
Ah, the rope!
Thud!

CLARE MARKET

In the market of Clare, so cheery the glare
Of the shops and the booths of the tradespeople there,
That I take a delight, on a Saturday night,
In walking that way and viewing the sight;
For it's here that one sees all the objects that please—
New patterns in silk and old patterns in cheese,
For the girls pretty toys, rude alarums for boys,
And baubles galore which discretion enjoys—
But here I forbear, for I really despair
Of naming the wealth of the market of Clare!

The rich man comes down from the elegant town,
And looks at it all with an ominous frown;
He seems to despise the grandiloquent cries
Of the vender proclaiming his puddings and pies;
And sniffing he goes through the lanes that disclose
Much cause for disgust to his sensitive nose;
Once free from the crowd, he admits that he is proud
That elsewhere in London this thing's not allowed—
He has seen nothing there but filth everywhere,
And he's glad to get out of the market of Clare.

But the child that has come from the neighboring slum
Is charmed by the magic of dazzle and hum;
He feasts his big eyes on the cakes and pies
And they seem to grow green and protrude with surprise
At the goodies they vend and the toys without end—
And it's oh if he had but a penny to spend!
But alas! he must gaze in a hopeless amaze
At treasures that glitter and torches that blaze—
What sense of despair in this world can compare
With that of the waif in the market of Clare?

So, on Saturday nights, when my custom invites
A stroll in old London for curious sights,
I am likely to stray by a devious way
Where goodies are spread in a motley array,
The things which some eyes would appear to despise
Impress me as pathos in homely disguise,
And my tattered waif friend shall have pennies to spend,
As long as I've got 'em (or friends that will lend);
And the urchin shall share in my joy and declare
That there's beauty and good in that marketplace there!

UNCLE EPHRAIM

My Uncle Ephraim was a man who did not live in vain,
And yet, why he succeeded so I never could explain;
By nature he was not endowed with wit to a degree,
But folks allowed there nowhere lived a better man than he;
He started poor but soon got rich; he went to congress then,
And held that post of honor long against much brainier men;
He never made a famous speech or did a thing of note,
And yet the praise of Uncle Eph welled up from every throat.

I recollect I never heard him say a bitter word;
He never carried to and fro unpleasant things he heard;
He always doffed his hat and spoke to every one he knew,
He tipped to poor and rich alike a genial "how-dy'-do";
He kissed the babies, praised their looks, and said: "That child will grow

To be a Daniel Webster or our president, I know!"
His voice was so mellifluous, his smile so full of mirth,
That folks declared he was the best and smartest man on earth!

Now, father was a smarter man, and yet he never won
Such wealth and fame as Uncle Eph, "the deestrick's favorite son";
He had "convictions" and he was not loath to speak his mind—
He went his way and said his say as he might be inclined;
Yes, he was brainy; yet his life was hardly a success—
He was too honest and too smart for this vain world, I guess!
At any rate, I wondered he was unsuccessful when
My Uncle Eph, a duller man, was so revered of men!

When Uncle Eph was dying he called me to his bed,
And in a tone of confidence inviolate he said:
"Dear Willyum, ere I seek repose in yonder blissful sphere
I fain would breathe a secret in your adolescent ear;
Strive not to hew your way through life—it really doesn't pay;
Be sure the salve of flattery soaps all you do and say!
Herein the only royal road to fame and fortune lies;
Put not your trust in vinegar—molasses catches flies!"

THIRTY-NINE

O hapless day! O wretched day!
I hoped you'd pass me by—
Alas, the years have sneaked away
And all is changed but I!
Had I the power, I would remand
You to a gloom condign,
But here you've crept upon me and
I—I am thirty-nine!

Now, were I thirty-five, I could
Assume a flippant guise,
Or, were I forty years, I should
Undoubtedly look wise;
For forty years are said to bring
Sedateness superfine,
But thirty-nine don't mean a thing—
A bas with thirty-nine!

You healthy, hulking girls and boys—
What makes you grow so fast?
Oh, I'll survive your lusty noise—
I'm tough and bound to last!
No, no—I'm old and withered, too—
I feel my powers decline.
(Yet none believes this can be true

Of one at thirty-nine.)

And you, dear girl with velvet eyes,
I wonder what you mean
Through all our keen anxieties
By keeping sweet sixteen.
With your dear love to warm my heart,
Wretch were I to repine—
I was but jesting at the start—
I'm glad I'm thirty-nine!

So, little children, roar and race
As blithely as you can
And, sweetheart, let your tender grace
Exalt the Day and Man;
For then these factors (I'll engage)
All subtly shall combine
To make both juvenile and sage
The one who's thirty-nine!

Yes, after all, I'm free to say
That I rejoice to be
Standing as I do stand to-day
'Twixt devil and deep sea;
For, though my face be dark with care
Or with a grimace shine,
Each haply falls unto my share;
Since I am thirty-nine!

'Tis passing meet to make good cheer
And lord it like a king,
Since only once we catch the year
That doesn't mean a thing.
O happy day! O gracious day!
I pledge thee in this wine—
Come let us journey on our way
A year, good Thirty-Nine!

HORACE I, 18

O Varus mine
Plant thou the vine
Within this kindly soil of Tibur;
Nor temporal woes
Nor spiritual knows
The man who's a discreet imbiber.
For who doth croak
Of being broke
Or who of warfare, after drinking?

With bowl atween us,
Of smiling Venus
And Bacchus shall we sing, I'm thinking.

Of symptoms fell
Which brawls impel
Historic data give us warning;
The wretch who fights
When full of nights
Is bound to have a head next morning.
I do not scorn
A friendly horn,
But noisy toots—I can't abide 'em!
Your howling bat
Is stale and flat
To one who knows, because he's tried 'em!

The secrets of
The life of love
(Companionship with girls and toddy)
I would not drag
With drunken brag
Into the ken of everybody,
But in the shade
Let some coy maid
With smilax wreathe my flagon's nozzle—
Then, all day long,
With mirth and song,
Shall I enjoy a quiet sozzle!

THREE RHINELAND DRINKING SONGS

I

If our life is the life of a flower
(And that's what some sages are thinking),
We should moisten the bud with a health-giving flood
And 'twill bloom all the sweeter—
Yes, life's the completer
For drinking,
and drinking,
and drinking!

If it be that our life is a journey
(As many wise folks are opining),
We should sprinkle the way with the rain while we may;
Though dusty and dreary,
'Tis made cool and cheery
With wining,

and wining,
and wining!

If this life that we live be a dreaming
(As pessimist people are thinking),
To induce pleasant dreams there is nothing, me seems,
Like this sweet prescription,
That baffles description—
This drinking,
and drinking,
and drinking!

II

("Fiducit")

Three comrades on the German Rhine—
Defying care and weather—
Together quaffed the mellow wine
And sung their songs together,
What recked they of the griefs of life
With wine and song to cheer them?
Though elsewhere trouble might be rife,
It would not come anear them!

Anon one comrade passed away,
And presently another—
And yet unto the tryst each day
Repaired the lonely brother,
And still, as gayly as of old,
That third one, hero-hearted,
Filled to the brim each cup of gold
And called to the departed:

"O comrades mine, I see you not,
Nor hear your kindly greeting;
Yet in this old familiar spot
Be still our loving meeting!
Here have I filled each bouting cup
With juices red and cherry—
I pray ye drink the portion up,
And, as of old, make merry!"

And once before his tear-dimmed eyes,
All in the haunted gloaming,
He saw two ghostly figures rise
And quaff the beakers foaming;
He heard two spirit voices call:
"Fiducit, jovial brother!"
And so forever from that hall

Went they with one another.

(Der Mann im Keller)

How cool and fair this cellar where
My throne a dusky cask is!
To do no thing but just to sing
And drown the time my task is!
The cooper, he's
Resolved to please,
And, answering to my winking,
He fills me up
Cup after cup
For drinking, drinking, drinking.

Begrudge me not this cozy spot
In which I am reclining—
Why, who would burst with envious thirst
When he can live by wining?
A roseate hue seems to imbue
The world on which I'm blinking;
My fellow men—I love them when
I'm drinking, drinking, drinking.

And yet, I think, the more I drink,
It's more and more I pine for—
Oh such as I (forever dry!)
God made this land of Rhine for!
And there is bliss
In knowing this,
As to the floor I'm sinking;
I've wronged no man,
And never can,
While drinking, drinking, drinking!

THE THREE TAILORS

(From the German of C. Herlossohn)

I shall tell you in rhyme how, once on a time,
Three tailors tramped up to the Inn Ingleheim
On the Rhine—lovely Rhine;
They were broke, but, the worst of it all, they were curst
With that malady common to tailors—a thirst
For wine—lots of wine!

"Sweet host," quoth the three, "we're as hard up as can be,
Yet skilled in the practice of cunning are we
On the Rhine—genial Rhine;
And we pledge you we will impart you that skill
Right quickly and fully, providing you'll fill
Us with wine—cooling wine!"

But that host shook his head, and warily said:
"Though cunning be good, we take money instead,
On the Rhine—thrifty Rhine;
If ye fancy ye may without pelf have your way
You'll find there's both host and the devil to pay
For your wine—costly wine!"

Then the first knavish wight took his needle so bright
And threaded its eye with a wee ray of light
From the Rhine—sunny Rhine;
And in such a deft way patched a mirror that day
That where it was mended no expert could say—
Done so fine—'twas for wine!

The second thereat spied a poor little gnat
Go toiling along on his nose broad and flat
Toward the Rhine—pleasant Rhine;
"Aha, tiny friend, I should hate to offend,
But your stockings need darning," which same did he mend,
All for wine—soothing wine!

And next there occurred what you'll deem quite absurd—
His needle a space in the wall thrust the third,
By the Rhine—wondrous Rhine;
And then, all so spry, he leapt through the eye
Of that thin cambric needle; nay, think you I'd lie
About wine? Not for wine!

The landlord allowed (with a smile) he was proud
To do the fair thing by that talented crowd
On the Rhine—generous Rhine!
So a thimble filled he as full as could be;
"Drink long and drink hearty, my jolly guests three,
Of my wine—filling wine!"

MORNING HYMN

I'd dearly love to tear my hair
And romp around a bit,
For I am mad enough to swear
Since Brother Chauncy quit.

I am so vilely prone to sin—
Vain ribald that I am—
I'd take a hideous pleasure in
Just one prodigious "damn."

But shall I yield to Satan's wiles
And let my passions swell?
Nay, I will wreath my face in smiles,
And mock the powers of hell.

And howsoever pride may roll
Its billows through my frame,
I'll not condemn my precious soul
Unto the quenchless flame!

But rather will I humbly pray
Divinity to wash
From out my mouth such words away
As "Jiminy" and "Gosh."

DOCTORS

'Tis quite the thing to say and sing
Gross libels on the doctor—
To picture him an ogre grim
Or humbug-pill concocter;
Yet it's in quite another light
My friendly pen would show him—
Glad that it might with verse repay
Some part of what I owe him!

When one's all right he's prone to spite
The doctor's peaceful mission;
But, when he's sick, it's loud and quick
He bawls for a physician!
With other things the doctor brings
Sweet babes our hearts to soften;
Though I have four, I pine for more—
Good doctor, pray, come often!

What though he sees death and disease
Run riot all around him,
Patient and true, and valorous, too—
Such have I always found him!
Where'er he goes he soothes our woes,
And, when skill's unavailing
And death is near, his words of cheer
Support our courage failing.

In ancient days they used to praise
The godlike art of healing;
An art that then engaged all men
Possessed of sense and feeling;
Why, Raleigh—he was glad to be
Famed for a quack elixir,
And Digby sold (as we are told)
A charm for folk love-sick, sir!

Napoleon knew a thing or two,
And clearly he was partial
To doctors, for, in time of war,
He chose one for marshal,
In our great cause a doctor was
The first to pass death's portal,
And Warren's name at once became
A beacon and immortal!

A heap, indeed, of what we read
By doctors is provided,
For to those groves Apollo loves
Their leaning is decided;
Deny who may that Rabelais
Is first in wit and learning—
And yet all smile and marvel while
His brilliant leaves they're turning.

How Lever's pen has charmed all men—
How touching Rab's short story!
And I will stake my all that Drake
Is still the schoolboy's glory!
A doctor-man it was began
Great Britain's great museum;
The treasures there are all so rare,
It drives me wild to see 'em!

There's Cuvier, Parr and Rush—they are
Big monuments to learning;
To Mitchell's prose (how smooth it flows!)
We all are fondly turning;
Tomes might be writ of that keen wit
Which Abernethy's famed for—
With bread-crumb pills he cured the ills
Most doctors get blamed for!

In modern times the noble rhymes
Of Holmes (a great physician!)
Have solace brought and wisdom taught
To hearts of all conditions.
The sailor bound for Puget sound
Finds pleasure still unfailing,

If he but troll the barcarole
Old Osborne wrote on Whaling!

If there were need I could proceed
Ad naus, with this prescription,
But, inter nos, a larger dose
Might give you fits conniption;
Yet, ere I end, there's one dear friend
I'd hold before these others,
For he and I in years gone by,
Have chummed around like brothers.

Together we have sung in glee
The songs old Horace made for
Our genial craft—together quaffed
What bowls that doctor paid for!
I love the rest, but love him best,
And, were not times so pressing,
I'd buy and send—you smile, old friend?
Well, then, here goes my blessing.

BEN APFELGARTEN

There was a certain gentleman, Ben Apfelgarten called,
Who lived way off in Germany a many years ago,
And he was very fortunate in being very bald,
And so was very happy he was so.
He warbled all the day
Such songs as only they
Who are very, very circumspect and very happy may;
The people wondered why,
As the years went grinding by,
They never heard him once complain or even heave a sigh!

The women of the province fell in love with genial Ben,
Till (maybe you can fancy it) the dickens was to pay
Among the callow students and the sober-minded men—
With the women folk a-cuttin' up that way!
Why, they gave him turbans red
To adorn his hairless head,
And knitted jaunty nightcaps to protect him when abed!
In vain the rest demurred—
Not a single chiding word
Those ladies deigned to tolerate—remonstrance was absurd!

Things finally got into such a very dreadful way
That the others (oh, how artful!) formed the politic design
To send him to the reichstag; so, one dull November day
They elected him a member from the Rhine!

Then the other members said:
"Gott in Himmel; what a head!"
But they marveled when his speeches they listened to or read;
And presently they cried:
"There must be heaps inside
Of the smooth and shiny cranium his constituents deride!"

Well, when at last he up 'nd died—long past his ninetieth year—
The strangest and the most luguberous funeral he had,
For women came in multitudes to weep upon his bier—
The men all wond'ring why on earth the women had gone mad!
And this wonderment increased,
Till the sympathetic priest
Inquired of those same ladies: "Why this fuss about deceased?"
Whereupon they were appalled,
For, as one, those women squalled:
"We doted on deceased for being bald—bald—bald!"

He was bald because his genius burnt that shock of hair away,
Which, elsewise, clogs one's keenness and activity of mind,
And (barring present company, of course,) I'm free to say
That, after all, it's intellect that captures woman-kind.
At any rate, since then
(With a precedent in Ben),
The women-folk have been in love with us bald-headed men!

IN HOLLAND

Our course lay up a smooth canal
Through tracks of velvet green,
And through the shade that windmills made,
And pasture lands between.
The kine had canvas on their backs
To temper Autumn's spite,
And everywhere there was an air
Of comfort and delight.

My wife, dear philosophic soul!
Saw here whereof to prate:
"Vain fools are we across the sea
To boast our nobler state!
Go north or south or east or west,
Or wheresoever you please,
You shall not find what's here combined—
Equality and ease!

"How tidy are these honest homes
In every part and nook—
The men folk wear a prosperous air,

The women happy look.
Seeing the peace that smiles around,
I would our land was such—
Think as you may, I'm free to say
I would we were the Dutch!"

Just then we overtook a boat
(The Golden Tulip hight)—
Big with the weight of motley freight,
It was a goodly sight!
Meynheer van Blarcom sat on deck,
With pipe in lordly pose,
And with his son of twenty-one
He played at dominoes.

Then quoth my wife: "How fair to see
This sturdy, honest man
Beguile all pain and lust of gain
With whatso joys he can;
Methinks his spouse is down below
Beading a kerchief gay—
A babe, mayhap, lolls in her lap
In the good old Milky way.

"Where in the land from whence we came
Is there content like this—
Where such disdain of sordid gain,
Such sweet domestic bliss?
A homespun woman I, this land
Delights me overmuch—
Think as you will and argue still,
I like the honest Dutch."

And then my wife made end of speech—
Her voice stuck in her throat,
For, swinging around the turn, we found
What motor moved the boat;
Hitched up in tow-path harness there
Was neither horse nor cow,
But the buxom frame of a Hollandische dame—
Meynheer van Blarcom's frau.

Eugene Field – A Short Biography

Eugene Field was born on 2nd September, 1850 in St. Louis, Missouri at 634 S. Broadway to parents Roswell Martin and Frances Reed Field, both of New England stock. Tragically Field lost his mother at age 6 and was thereafter brought up by a cousin, Mary Field French, in Amherst, Massachusetts.

Field attended Williams College in Williamstown, Massachusetts.

When he was 19 his father died, and Field dropped out of Williams. Field's father, Roswell Martin Field, was the lawyer for Dred Scott, the slave who famously sued for his freedom. The complaint was sometimes referred to as 'The lawsuit that started the Civil War'.

Field then went to Knox College in Galesburg, Illinois, but again dropped out. This time after a year. However he did then summon himself to attend the University of Missouri in Columbia, Missouri, where his brother Roswell was studying. As can be gathered from his efforts to date Field was not the most serious of students but was gaining the reputation of being a prankster. Among his more outlandish attempts were a raid on the president's wine cellar, painting the president's house in school colors, and firing the school's landmark cannons at midnight.

Field tried acting but found it not to his liking, studied law but with little success, but did have an interest in writing for the student newspaper.

When his studies finished in 1871, although he never graduated, he collected his share of his inheritance from his father's estate, and set off for a trip to explore Europe. After six months, with funds from the inheritance exhausted, he returned to the United States.

Field then set to work as a journalist for the St. Joseph Gazette in Saint Joseph, Missouri, in 1875.

That same year he married the sixteen-year-old Julia Sutherland Comstock of St Joseph, Missouri. They would eventually have eight children during their twenty-two years of marriage, of whom only five would reach adulthood. Field, knowing that his understanding of finances was somewhat poor, arranged for all the money he earned to be sent to his wife for her to administer on behalf of the family.

In his career as a journalist he soon found a niche that suited him. His articles were light, humorous and written in a personal and gossipy style that endeared him to his readership. Some were soon being syndicated to other newspapers around the States. Field rose to be the city editor of the Gazette.

From 1876 through 1880, the Family lived in St. Louis. Field worked initially as an editorial writer for the Morning Journal and then for the Times-Journal. From there he worked for a short time as the managing editor of the Kansas City Times before settling, for two years, as the editor of the Denver Tribune. He also wrote a column for the paper, 'Odds and Ends,' poking fun at the climate, the muddy roads, the frontier language, and other aspects of Denver life. However his readership was large and growing. Further opportunities would come.

In 1883 the Field moved the family to Chicago lured by a salary of $50 a week. Field now began work for the Chicago Daily News. Here he wrote his humorous newspaper column called Sharps and Flats. He quickly found out that $50 dollars in Denver didn't stretch that far in bustling Chicago.

His column ran in the newspaper's morning edition. In it Field made quips about issues and personalities of the day, especially regarding the arts and literature. His pet subject was the intellectual superiority of Chicago, especially when he compared it to Boston, which he often did. In April 1887, he wrote, "While Chicago is humping herself in the interests of literature, art and the sciences, vain old Boston is frivoling away her precious time in an attempted renaissance of the cod fisheries."

In another article that year after Chicago's National League baseball club sold future baseball Hall of Famer Mike "King" Kelly to Boston which overlapped with a speaking tour visit from the famous Boston poet and diplomat James Russell Lowell he wrote: "Chicago feels a special interest in Mr. Lowell at this particular time because he is perhaps the foremost representative of the enterprising and opulent community which within the last week has secured the services of one of Chicago's honored sons for the base-ball season of 1887. The fact that Boston has come to Chicago for the captain of her baseball nine has reinvigorated the bonds of affection between the metropolis of the Bay state and the metropolis of the mighty west; the truth of this will appear in the mighty welcome which our public will give Mr. Lowell next Tuesday."

It was in 1888 that his poem 'Little Boy Blue' was printed in America, a weekly journal. It achieved for Field instant and lasting fame. Coincidentally the same issue carried a poem by James Russell Lowell. Field was immensely pleased that his own poem was regarded with considerably more weight and acclaim.

Field had first published poetry in 1879, when his poem 'Christmas Treasures' was published. It later appeared in 'A Little Book of Western Verse' (1889). This was the beginning that would eventually number over a dozen volumes. He developed a style of light-hearted poems for children. Among the perennial favorites are 'Wynken, Blynken, and Nod' and 'The Duel' (but better known as 'The Gingham Dog and the Calico Cat') and 'Little Boy Blue' about the death of a child. As well as verse Field published an extensive range of short stories including 'The Holy Cross' and 'Daniel and the Devil.'

Field treasured rare, unusual and beautiful books and his personal library had scores of them. He also enjoyed making them too and frequently worked long hours with great care and various colored inks decorating the first letter of his poems.

In 1889 whilst the family were in London and Field himself was recovering from a bout of ill health he wrote his most famous poem; 'Lovers Lane'. It is often thought to have been written whilst the couple were courting but recent research settles it authorship to this later date. The poem was written as a reminder of better days when the couple courted in her father's buggy on 'Lover's Lane, St Jo'.

Field was ever curious and keen to push his boundaries. In 1891 with his brother Roswell they wrote and published 'Echoes from the Sabine Farm' a loosely translated version of Horace.

On 4th November 1895 Eugene Field Sr died in Chicago of a heart attack at the age of 45. He is buried at the Church of the Holy Comforter in Kenilworth, Illinois.

The New York Times described his death: CHICAGO, Nov. 4. — Eugene Field, the poet and humorist, died at 5 o'clock this morning of heart disease at his residence in Buena Park. Although Mr. Field had been ill for the past three days, his sudden death was totally unexpected.

Field was originally interred at Graceland Cemetery in Chicago, but his son-in-law, Senior Warden of the Church of the Holy Comforter, had him reinterred on 7th March, 1926.

Several of his poems were set to music with commercial success. Many of his works were accompanied by paintings from the exceptional talents of Maxfield Parrish.

During his lifetime he was often referred to as the 'poet of childhood'. This may account for his anonymous publication of 'Only a Boy'. In our own times the work would probably be frowned upon. It concerns a 12-year-old boy being seduced by a woman in her 30s. The 1920's drama critic/magazine editor George Jean Nathan claimed it was a popular but forbidden work among those coming of age in the early 1900's.

Much of what Field wrote was light, humourous and of its time. And that is perhaps why it has endured. Its writes of a time that, in his words, suspends itself from the harsh reality of real life to a gentler and more touching time that exists in the imagination.

Eugene Field – A Concise Bibliography

The Tribune Primer (1882)
Culture's Garland (1887)
A Little Book of Profitable Tales (1889)
A Little Book of Western Verse (1889)
With Trumpet and Drum (1892)
Echoes from the Sabine Farm (1893)
The Holy Cross and Other Tales (1893)
Second Book of Verse (1893)
Love Songs of Childhood (1894)
Love Affairs of a Bibliomaniac (1895)
Little Willie (1895)
Songs and Other Verse (1896)
Second Book of Tales (1896)
The House; An Episode in the Lives of Reuben Baker, Astronomer and His Wife Alice (1896)
Field Flowers (1896)
Florence Bardsley's Story (1897)
Lullaby Songs of Childhood (1897)
Lullaby Land (1898)
Sharps and Flats (1900)
The Stars (1901)
Nonsense for Old and Young (1901)
A Little Book of Nonsense (1901)
A Little Book of Tribune Verse (1901)
The Sabine Farm (1903)
John Smith USA (1905)
The Clink of Ice (1905)
Hoosier Lyrics (1905)
Cradle Lullabies (1909)
The Poems of Eugene Field (1910)
Christmas Tales and Christmas Verse (1912)
Penn-Yan Bill's Wooing (1914)
The Yankee Abroad (1917)
The Mouse and the Moonbeam (1919)
Poems of Childhood (1920)
The Gingham Dog and the Calico Cat (1926)
Child Verses (1927)
The Sugar Plum Tree (1929)
In Wink-a-way Land (1930)